STAND UP: Bullying Prevention

What to Do When Your BROTHER or SISTER Is a BULLY

Addy Ferguson

PowerKiDS press.

New York

Published in 2015 by The Rosen Publishing Group, Inc.
29 East 21st Street, New York, NY 10010

First Edition

Editor: Jennifer Way
Book Design: Erica Clendening and Colleen Bialecki
Book Layout: Andrew Povolny
Photo Research: Katie Stryker

Photo Credits: Cover, p. 1 Fotosearch/Getty Images; p. 4 Elegor/Shutterstock.com; p. 5 BananaStock/ Thinkstock; p. 6; Fuse/Thinkstock; p. 7 Klaus Vedfelt/Iconica/Getty Images; p. 8 Creatas/Thinkstock; p. 9 Jeffrey Coolidge/Digital Vision/Getty Images; p. 11 shvili/iStock/Thinkstock; p. 12 Robert Hoetink/ Shutterstock.com; p. 13 DAJ/Thinkstock; p. 15 Tetra Images/Getty Images; p. 16 Wavebreakmedia Ltd/ Thinkstock; p. 17 Todd Wright/Blend Images/Thinkstock; p. 19 Thinkstock/Stockbyte/Thinkstock; p. 20 Diego Cervo/Shutterstock.com; p. 21 JGI/Jamie Grill/Blend Images/Getty Images; p. 22 Monkey Business Images/Shutterstock.com.

Library of Congress Cataloging-in-Publication Data

Ferguson, Addy.
 What to do when your brother or sister is a bully / by Addy Ferguson. — 1st ed.
    pages cm. — (Stand up : bullying prevention)
 Includes index.
 ISBN 978-1-4777-6898-3 (library binding) — ISBN 978-1-4777-6896-9 (pbk.) —
ISBN 978-1-4777-6621-7 (6-pack)
 1. Bullying—Juvenile literature. 2. Brothers and sisters—Juvenile literature. 3. Family violence—Juvenile literature. I. Title.
 BF637.B85F47185 2015
 302.34'3—dc23

                              2014004348

Manufactured in the United States of America

CPSIA Compliance Information: Batch #WS14PK5: For Further Information contact Rosen Publishing, New York, New York at 1-800-237-9932

Contents

What Is Bullying?

Bullying is a big problem in our communities. More than one-third of elementary-school students report being bullied at some point. The numbers grow even larger in later grades.

A bully can target someone over email, text, or social media. This is called cyberbullying.

Bullies single out kids they view as weaker than they are. They know they have more power over that kid and use that power to hurt others.

What is bullying? Bullying is **aggressive** behavior by someone with more power than another person. A bully may be bigger, stronger, or more popular than the person he bullies. Bullying is also behavior that happens over and over again.

Unfortunately, bullying doesn't just happen at school. It can happen on sports teams, the bus, at a public playground, and even at home by brothers and sisters.

Bullying in the Family

You and your brother or sister may fight sometimes. You may tease each other or say mean things. This can be normal **sibling** behavior. Normal teasing stops when the person being teased says he or she has had enough. However, if one sibling targets another and tries to hurt, **taunt**, or scare her repeatedly, it is bullying.

Even siblings who get along well will argue sometimes. Arguing occasionally is not bullying.

Normal teasing ends before feelings or bodies are hurt. When the taunting doesn't stop, that is bullying.

It can be difficult to spot bullying in a family because disagreements among family members can be common. If you feel your sibling might be bullying you, trust your **instincts** and ask for help.

Why Do Siblings Bully?

Siblings sometimes argue over things that they share. A brother who bullies might not let his sister watch a TV show that she wants to watch.

You might wonder why a sibling would bully you. People who bully generally want to feel powerful. Hurting another person, either **physically** or with words, gives them this feeling.

An older brother has more power than a younger one. He can use this power to hurt his sibling. He may feel the younger sibling gets more attention from a parent. He may enjoy making a sibling upset by teasing him or breaking or taking something that belongs to him. He may try to get him in trouble with a parent for something he did not do. No matter why a sibling bullies, bullying is always wrong.

A sibling might bully because she is jealous of the attention her sister gets for her good grades.

Is It Abuse?

Just because your brother or sister hurts you in anger sometimes does not make it **abuse**. It becomes abuse when verbal and physical attacks happen repeatedly and are generally **unprovoked**. If you are afraid to be alone with a sibling, then the relationship is likely an abusive one.

Sometimes siblings who bully their brothers or sisters are themselves bullied or abused by other people. Their bullies might be parents or older siblings, or they could be classmates or teammates. This does not make it okay for them to bully, though.

Sometimes kids say or do things to their sibling to guarantee that a fight will start. This is called provoking. Provoking does not excuse bullying, though.

The Effects of Bullying

You deserve to feel safe at home. If you are bullied by a sibling, you might not feel safe. This can make you feel isolated or scared.

Bullying has a lasting impact. Bullied people often feel **isolated**, scared, angry, and **depressed**. They feel helpless to make the bullying stop.

When bullying happens at school, the bullied person may feel that her only safe place is at home. However, when her bully is a sibling, there is no place to escape. This can make the bad feelings surrounding being bullied even worse. There can also be deep sadness and **resentment** that a family member has hurt her.

Parents sometimes do not understand that the behavior between siblings has gone past normal fighting or teasing. This can make the bullied child feel hurt, too.

When you are being bullied, you might find it harder to focus at school because you are worried about dealing with your bullying sibling.

Don't Fight Your Sibling

It can be hard to avoid a bully who lives in your home. You may even share the same bedroom. If your sibling bullies you, firmly tell him to leave you alone or ignore him. You can also walk away. If you can, go into a room that has an adult in it. Your sibling is unlikely to bully you where she can get caught.

Do not fight your sibling. You could get hurt. Your parent may also see the fighting and not the cause. Instead of solving your problem, you could end up in trouble.

Fighting is wrong. Your parents might punish both you and your sibling for fighting and not want to hear the reason the fight started.

Talking to Your Parents

If a sibling is bullying you, it is important that you talk to a parent. Explain what is happening. You should also tell your parent how your brother or sister is making you feel. Say you are afraid to be alone with her because her treatment of you is so bad.

Try talking to your father in private. Tell him that your sibling is bullying you. Give some examples of what is being done or said.

Some parents believe that fighting between siblings is a normal part of growing up. Explain to your parents that the fighting has crossed the line into bullying.

It may be hard for a parent to understand at first. Parents want to believe the best of all their children. They may also think that fighting and mean behavior is normal for brothers and sisters. Explain that what is happening is more than that. Ask them for help in making the behavior stop.

Talk to Another Adult

If your parents do not believe you, you may need to talk to another trusted adult. This might be a relative, teacher, coach, or school **counselor**. It might be easier for a person who does not live in your home to understand the problem. This other adult might also be able to explain to your parents that your sibling's behavior has moved past normal behavior into bullying.

An adult can help you think of ways to stay safe and put a stop to the bullying. She may be able to sit down with you and your sibling and help you both talk things through.

A trusted adult such as a coach might be able to help you deal with bullying. He might talk to your parents to explain how you are being bullied by a sibling.

Self-Esteem and Bullying

One of the main effects of bullying is to a person's self-esteem. Self-esteem is the way in which you see yourself. When you have high self-esteem, you like yourself and can see the good things in yourself.

A person who is bullied can start to suffer from **low self-esteem**. That person starts to feel bad about herself. She may start to believe that she deserves to be bullied.

When you have high self-esteem, you feel like you deserve to be happy and safe.

Do not let your brother or sister hurt your self-esteem. The mean things your bullying sibling says to you are not true. Your bullying sibling is trying to hurt you, but you do not have to let him or her succeed.

Low self-esteem can lead to feelings of worthlessness. This might make you less likely to seek help for bullying.

Healthy Relationships

A family member does not have the right to hurt you. Your home should be a safe place where everyone loves, trusts, and respects one another.

Have your whole family work on an action plan for becoming a bully-free family. Your family can get help from a counselor. A counselor can help your family change the behavior patterns that are allowing the bullying to continue. The most important thing to remember is that no one deserves to be bullied.

In a bully-free family, everyone respects one another. All members learn to work through disagreements without hurting each other.

Glossary

abuse (uh-BYOOS) Treating someone in a harmful way.

aggressive (uh-GREH-siv) Ready to fight.

counselor (KOWN-seh-ler) A person to whom someone can talk about his or her feelings.

depressed (dih-PRESD) Felt very sad for a long time.

instincts (IN-stinkts) Feelings all creatures have that help them know what to do.

isolated (EYE-suh-layt-ed) Placed apart and alone.

low self-esteem (LOH SELF-uh-STEEM) Not having pride or respect for yourself. Children with low self-esteem feel people are always judging them.

physically (FIH-zih-klee) Using the body.

resentment (rih-ZENT-ment) A feeling of having a grudge against someone for real or imagined wrongdoing.

sibling (SIH-bling) A person's sister or brother.

taunt (TAWNT) To tease repeatedly with the purpose of hurting or upsetting someone.

unprovoked (un-pruh-VOHKT) Did not stir up feelings on purpose.

Index

A
attacks, 10
attention, 9

C
communities, 4
counselor,
    18, 22

F
family, 7, 22
feeling(s), 8, 12

H
help, 7, 17, 22

I
instincts, 7

L
low self-esteem, 20

P
playground, 5
power, 5, 9

R
resentment, 12

S
students, 4

T
teams, 5
teasing, 6, 13

W
words, 8

Websites

Due to the changing nature of Internet links, PowerKids Press has developed an online list of websites related to the subject of this book. This site is updated regularly. Please use this link to access the list: www.powerkidslinks.com/subp/bro/